MW00635472

ADVENTURES IN ANDALUSIA

Top 10 Destinations

In Southern SPAIN

Liz Marino

COPYRIGHT

CONTENTS

CONTENTS

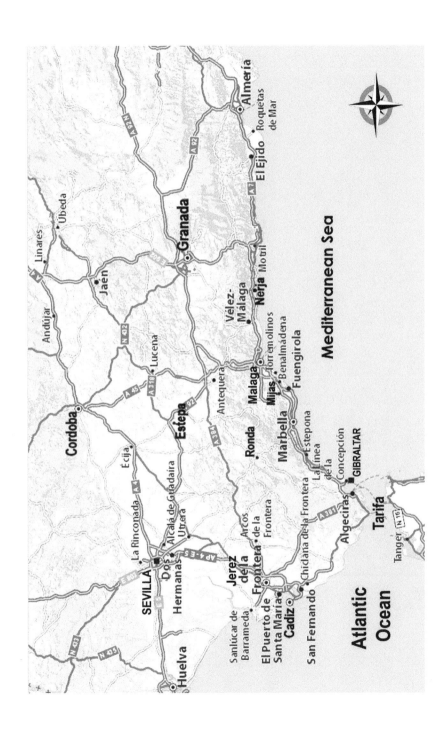

ANDALUSIA

White-washed villages, patios filled with flowers, the sounds of flamenco guitar, the scent of orange blossoms...these are just some of the sights and sensations that attract visitors to Andalusia.

Andalusia offers a wealth of history, mouth-watering gastronomy and a unique culture in a natural setting bordered by the Mediterranean and the Atlantic Ocean. Best of all, this region of Spain is one of the most affordable travel destinations in Western Europe.

This book is aimed at readers and travellers who seek an authentic and memorable experience in Southern Spain.

Correct Spelling?

Is it Andalusia or Andalucía? The correct spelling depends on what language you are writing in.

When writing in Spanish the correct spelling is **Andalucía**. In English it's **Andalusia**.

The name "Andalusia" is derived from the Arabic word Al-Andalus which in turn originates from Vandalusia or "land of the Vandals".

1-GRANADA

The Alhambra in Granada

Few places in Spain have managed to capture the imagination of as many poets, writers and artists as Granada.

Sitting at the feet of the **Sierra Nevada** mountains and overlooked by a magnificent palace, Granada is one of Europe's top travel destinations.

The Alhambra offer visitors a glimpse of Spain's Moorish past, a period that lasted some 800 years and ended in 1492, when Kings Ferdinand and Isabella recaptured the city from Boabdil, Granada's last Moorish king. The Alhambra is a fortress and a palace.

Today, Granada is a happy town with a bustling community.

The **University of Granada** adds a dose of energy to this lively city and attracts students from all over the world.

The Albayzin

The Albayzin Quarter

The Albayzin district, built on a hill and facing the Alhambra, was the first settlement in Granada. This ancient quarter was designated a UNESCO site in 1994.

The best place to view the Alhambra and the Sierra Nevada is the **Mirador de San Nicolas**, a lookout point in the Albayzin where people gather every day to see the ancient palace change colors, giving off its characteristic red tones from the light reflected by the Sun.

Plaza Larga is a lively square in the heart of the Albayzin with several shops, bars and restaurants.

The 15th-century **Palacio de Dar Al-Horra**, located near the **Plaza de San Miguel Bajo**, was the home of Boabdil's mother, (the last Muslim ruler of Granada).

This Moorish villa was inspired by the Alhambra, with a double patio porch, central hall and a lookout tower at one end. The panoramic views of the city from the tower are superb.

The Sacromonte

The **Sacromonte** (Sacred Mountain) is the old gypsy quarter located next to the Albayzin and deserves special mention. This small community of white-washed homes and caves attracts visitors for its nightly live flamenco performances and views of the Alhambra.

Since the 19th century, the caves of Sacromonte have entertained world celebrities, political figures and European jet setters.

Many of the caves have been restored and refurbished with modern conveniences for the use of tourists and local residents. The temperature inside these caves remains constant throughout the year, even during the hot summer months.

Granada's flamenco scene is raw, improvised and passionate. To experience an intimate performance inside a cave, I highly recommend a flamenco show in the Sacromonte.

GRANADA ATTRACTIONS

Besides the Alhambra, the Albayzin and Sacromonte quarters, Granada offers plenty of walking, shopping and sightseeing.

The **Paseo de los Tristes** is a long cobblestone street that runs parallel to the river Darro with several bars, restaurants, magnificent historic hotels and tourist shops.

Plaza Nueva, located next to Paseo de los Tristes, is a festive and busy square lined with hotels, restaurants, bars, ice cream and souvenir shops.

Not far from Plaza Nueva is the old **Realejo** quarter, ideal for walking and sightseeing.

In el Realejo, near **Calle Molinos**, you'll see **Campo del Principe**, a family friendly park and playground with several tapas bars. The park is located at the foot of a hill with amazing views of historic homes and cypress trees. At the top of the hill sits the **Alhambra Palace** hotel.

Returning to the city on **Gran Via de Colon** street, is Granada's **Cathedral** and **Royal Chapel**, a key landmark and the final resting place of Kings Isabella and Ferdinand.

Just a short walk from the Cathedral is the **Plaza Bib Rambla**, a good place to enjoy an outdoor lunch or dinner and try some *churros con chocolate*. Visitors will several find several souvenir and handcraft shops in this area.

Tip

Granada is small enough to explore on foot or by bus. Walking in Granada is a smart option since parking is expensive or non-existent and streets are very narrow.

How to purchase tickets to the Alhambra

Tickets can be purchased in several ways:

1. At the ticket office located in the Alhambra. (Expect long lines).

2. Via the Internet by visiting www.ticketmaster.es

3. By taking a guided tour (highly recommended)

4. Through an authorized travel agency

Getting There

Several international carriers fly into Malaga, Madrid and Barcelona. Malaga, the closest city to Granada, is less than 90 minutes away by bus.

Since there are many more flights to Malaga than to Granada, many people fly to Malaga and then catch a bus or hire a car.

If you fly into Madrid a bus trip to Granada takes 5 hours.

2-ESTEPA

View from the Castle of Estepa

Estepa is a white Andalusian village, built on the side of a mountain, with a superb geographic location and amazing scenery.

Sitting high on a plateau in the heart of Andalusia, the town offers panoramic views of a rich agricultural region, where vast fields of olive trees extend as far as the eye can see.

Estepa has several historic monuments, including an ancient castle and a baroque style tower, named **Torre de la Victoria**, rising above every other building in town.

ESTEPA ATTRACTIONS

The **Castillo de Estepa** overlooks the town and offers spectacular views of the surrounding countryside.

In addition to olive oil, Estepa is famous for its *mantecados*, a traditional Andalusian shortbread made from flour, sugar, milk and nuts.

Many local families take part in the production of this product at one of 20 plus family-owned factories.

Another place to visit in Estepa is the **Museo del Chocolate** or **Choco Mundo** (located next to La Despensa de Palacio) where visitors can sample hot chocolate and other sweets while learning about the history of chocolate.

The **Balcon de Andalucia** (Hotel and Restaurant) is very popular with tourists and locals and serves traditional Andalusian food.

Getting There

When driving through Andalusia, the town of **Estepa** is located one hour from **Seville**, one hour from **Cordoba**, one hour from **Granada** and one hour from **Malaga** making it a convenient stop over between any of those cities. Driving distance to **Ronda** is 90 minutes.

3-CORDOBA

Mezquita of Cordoba

Cordoba became the capital of Al-Andalus in 716, following the Moorish occupation of Spain in 711.

The most impressive legacy left by the Moors in this city is the famous Mezquita, one of the biggest mosques in the world. This mosque was built between the years 780 to 785 AD over a Christian Visigoth church.

By the 10th century, Cordoba had become a city of great wealth and enlightenment during Europe's Dark Ages. The Mezquita was a place of worship and one of the leading centers of higher education in the world at the time.

Cordoba's Mosque-Cathedral is a UNESCO World Heritage Site.

Cordoba's Mezquita features various styles of Arabic art while the column capitals reveal Visigoth, Roman, Gothic and Baroque influences.

In 1236 King **Fernando III** of Castile gained control of Cordoba from the Moors. After the Christian Reconquest, the mosque was converted and consecrated as a cathedral.

Beyond its rich architectural past, Cordoba is a modern city with fine hotels and a multitude of festivals and cultural events.

Within walking distance of the Mezquita, visitors will find plenty of shops selling quality leather goods, ceramics and other crafts.

CORDOBA ATTRACTIONS

The **Bridge** over the **Guadalquivir** is one of the city's main attractions. This Moorish bridge was built on the foundations of an ancient Roman bridge.

The bridge runs from the Torre (Tower) de la Calahorra on the south and ends on the north side of the river, just a block from the Mezquita.

The **Alcazar de los Reyes Cristianos**, (Castle of the Christian Monarchs) was built in 1328 and was used as a residence by several Catholic kings, during the *Reconquista*.

It was in this palace that Christopher Columbus explained his plans for a sea voyage to Ferdinand and Isabella in 1486.

Today, visitors can tour the palace, wander through its gardens and climb to a tower to view the city.

The **Calleja de las Flores**, located near the Mosque, is a narrow alleyway with white walls and flowers on both sides, and one of the most beautiful streets in Cordoba.

Bridge over Guadalquivir

The **Jewish Quarter** *(Judería)* with its narrow, picturesque streets, charming homes and a 14th century synagogue is the best known part of the historic center, just two blocks west of the Mezquita.

At one time this was the biggest Jewish community in Europe.

El Zoco, located in the Jewish quarter, is a group of small workshops where visitors can watch artisans turn raw materials into unique handmade ceramics, jewelry and leather crafts. This is a good place to buy gifts and souvenirs.

Plaza de las Tendillas is the city's main square, surrounded by 19th century buildings and several bars and cafes.

The square features two fountains and a large statue of Gonzalo Fernandez de Cordoba, better known as **El Gran Capitán**.

For 600 years, up until the 5th century AD, Cordoba was a Roman city, as evidenced by the rich architectural legacy still present that includes a necropolis, several ancient walls and the bridge over the Guadalquivir.

History buffs will enjoy a visit to the **Museo Arqueológico de Cordoba**. Built over the excavated remains of a Roman amphitheater, the museum houses a collection of artifacts from prehistoric times to the period of the Moors. The museum is located near the **Plaza de las Tendillas**.

Tip

Cordoba is mostly flat. The city's narrow streets are ideal for walking or bicycling. From April to October the Tourism Office offers a series of guided walks.

Getting There

There are no direct flights to Cordoba but **Malaga**, **Seville** and **Madrid** are less than 2 hours away by high speed (AVE) train. Driving time from **Granada** to **Cordoba** is about 2 hours and 24 minutes.

Driving Distances

Cordoba - Seville	109 km / 68 miles
Cordoba - Granada	208 km / 129 miles
Cordoba - Malaga	163 km / 101 miles

4-RONDA

"El Tajo", Ronda

Sitting on a high plateau, the city of Ronda is a natural fortress facing the **Sierra de Grazalema** mountains. The Celts aptly named the city *Arunda* which means "surrounded by mountains".

It is difficult to find a photo that fully captures the majestic and impressive sights of Ronda. The gap shown in the photo, known as "*el Tajo*" in Spanish, was carved by constant erosion from the Guadalevin river.

The **Puente Nuevo** (new bridge) crosses the gorge at its closest point and reaches a height of 98 meters from the bottom of the ravine.

The bridge connects the old Moorish quarters with the modern town known as **El Mercadillo** (the little market).

RONDA ATTRACTIONS

There is enough to do and see in Ronda to justify staying one or two nights. Visitors should at least try to stay long enough to witness a sunset or a sunrise from this magnificent city.

Waterfall in "El Tajo"

Trails Along the Gorge

Nature lovers will find easy hiking trails along the gorge with great views of the waterfalls, the bridge and the countryside.

15

Casa Don Bosco

This small palace is located in the heart of the old town and right on the edge of the gorge. Its gardens and interiors are well worth a visit.

Moorish Baths

The Moorish baths of Ronda are considered to be some of the best preserved in Spain. The vaulted ceiling features star shaped skylights. An English film explains the history of the baths. The baths are located in what is currently known as the **San Miguel** quarter.

La Casa Del Rey Moro

The "House of the Moorish King", built in the 18th century, is not really Moorish except for its ancient water mine, an authentic reminder of Ronda's history.

Visitors can descend to the underground mine from the garden. For those who can handle the stairs this is an amazing place to see and experience.

Travel Tip

Ronda is a small town, easy to explore on foot. The two highways that link Ronda to Costa del Sol have several twists and turns. For this reason, it is best to avoid arriving or leaving at night whenever possible.

Trivia

Ernest Hemingway spent many summers in Ronda primarily for its bullfights, which he referenced in at least two of his novels. The **Paseo de Hemingway** pathway in Ronda is named in his honor.

Ronda is the final resting place of film director **Orson Welles**. Two years after he passed away in 1985, his ashes were flown to Spain and laid to rest in a farm owned by his friend, Antonio Ordoñez, on the outskirts of Ronda.

Getting There

Driving from the coast to Ronda takes about 90 minutes. Ronda can be reached by train or bus.

Driving Distances

Ronda - Marbella	60 km / 37.5 miles
Ronda - Malaga	105 km / 65 miles
Ronda - Seville	132 km / 82 miles
Ronda - Cadiz	154 km / 96 miles

5-SEVILLE

Torre del Oro in Seville

Seville is the capital and most stately city of Andalusia. Its strategic location along the Guadalquivir has been a key factor in this city's economic development for centuries.

As a key trading center with Spain's American colonies, Seville became one of Europe's grand cities in the 16th century.

Seville today is one of the most affluent cities in Andalusia, with several thriving industries besides tourism. Its traditional fiestas attract thousands of visitors each year.

The **Feria de Sevilla** takes place in the later part of April, a lavish celebration of music, fancy horse riders and women dressed in colorful flamenco dresses.

The **Avenida Constitución** runs through the center of town and is lined with banks, shops and cafes.

On the northern end of this avenue is **Plaza Nueva** square, which borders the city's main shopping district.

At the center of this plaza, a monument honors **King Fernando III**, who freed Seville from the Moors in 1248. (This is the same King Fernando who seized control of Cordoba in 1236).

SEVILLE ATTRACTIONS

The **Guadalquivir** separates the city into two sections, leaving most of the historic attractions on the eastern side of the river.

The **Alcazar de Sevilla** is a beautiful Moorish fortress that now functions as a part-time residence for the Spanish royal family.

Seville's grand **Cathedral**, built over a mosque, is the third largest church in Europe. The tomb of **Cristopher Columbus** is located inside the cathedral. (His remains are believed to have been sent from Havana to Seville in 1902).

One of Seville's most famous monuments is the **Giralda** tower. Originally a Moorish minaret, the Giralda, now functions as the cathedral's bell tower. The tower offers great views of the city.

Another main attraction in Seville is the **Plaza de España**, an impressive, semi-circular building complex with towers at either end. In front of the building, there's a canal crossed by four bridges, with the Plaza in its center.

Maria Luisa Park in Seville

The Plaza is located in **Maria Luisa Park,** named after Princess **Maria Luisa de Orleans**, who donated half of the gardens to the city in 1893.

The city's second most famous monument is the **Torre del Oro**, built on the banks of the Guadalquivir in the 13th century. Visitors can enter the tower and climb to the top where the city views are stunning.

Across the Guadalquivir is the **Triana district**, a lively sector of Seville, famous for its flamenco bars and ceramic shops. In the Triana district, visitors can wonder through the many shops that line the streets and find traditional ceramics made by local artists.

Seville's **Museum of Fine Arts** is the second largest art gallery in Spain after the Prado Museum in Madrid.

The museum offers a rich collection of paintings from Spain's Golden Age that includes religious and Baroque works from several Spanish artists. The building that houses the museum is magnificent.

Travel Tip

Walking is a great way to explore Seville. A motor vehicle is only necessary to travel outside the city.

In addition to bike tours and private bike rentals the city offers a public bike rental service called *Sevici*. There are several public bike stations located throughout the city.

Getting There

Seville San Pablo Airport is located on the A4 highway that connects Seville to **Madrid**. The motorways around Seville provide easy access to **Jerez**, **Malaga** and **Cadiz**.

A bus ride from the airport to the centre of Seville takes about 40 minutes.

Driving Distances

Seville – Jerez	90 km / 56 miles
Seville – Cordoba	140 km / 87 miles
Seville – Cadiz	126 km / 78 miles
Seville – Malaga	216 km / 134 miles

6-CADIZ

Cadiz

Located on the southwestern portion of Spain, just two hours away from Seville and Ronda, the city of **Cadiz** combines the excitement of a port city with historic architecture and a laid-back atmosphere.

With 3,000 years of recorded history, Cadiz is considered the oldest continuously inhabited city in the country and the most ancient city of Western Europe. Christopher Columbus sailed from the port of Cadiz on his fourth and final trip to the New World in 1502.

CADIZ ATTRACTIONS

Parque Genoves, Cadiz

Cadiz **Old Town** (*Casco Histórico*) offers plenty of walking opportunities for visitors. Tourists will find tapa bars, tiny boutiques and small shops while strolling through a maze of blind alleys and cobblestone streets.

The **Alameda de Apodaca** park stretches between the old city walls and the sea and offers a pleasant walking experience along the coast. This is a great place for sunset viewing.

Facing the Alameda is **Parque Genoves**, a family-friendly park with a great collection of rare trees and exotic plants from all over the world. Children can enjoy the grotto area complete with a waterfall and a playground.

The Old Town is best known for its vast number of historic buildings, forts, watchtowers and the 18th century **Catedral de la Santa Cruz** (or Catedral Nueva), famous for its golden dome.

The **Plaza de la Mina**, in the heart of the Old Town, where the **Cadiz Museum** is located, is one of the most beautiful squares in Cadiz.

The **Cadiz Museum** showcases archeological artifacts from the Phoenician, Punic and Roman periods and a collection of paintings dating from the 16th to the 20th centuries.

The **Tavira Tower** is the biggest watchtower in Cadiz. Tourists can climb to the top of the tower and admire the best views of the city and the Bay of Cadiz.

At one end of the **Caleta** beach is the **Castle of San Sebastian** which used to be a military fort. The castle can be reached by walking through a causeway.

Beaches

Cadiz has fine beaches like **Santa Maria del Mar**, **Victoria** and **Cortadura**. Santa Maria del Mar is a continuation of Victoria beach and begins between the old and the new side of Cadiz. It is the next beach after **La Caleta**.

Heading further south, tourists can explore other beaches along the coastline like **Chiclana** and **Conil de la Frontera**. The clear waters of the Atlantic offer great swimming and surfing.

Nearest Town

Just 35 minutes from Cadiz, heading north, is the town of **Jerez de la Frontera**, famous for its production of **Jerez** (Sherry) and its Royal Andalusian **School of Equestrian Art**, world renowned for its dancing stallions shows.

Travel Tip

Cadiz is mostly flat and can be easily explored on foot or on a bicycle.

Getting There

The quickest way to get to Cadiz is through **La Parra International Airport**, in Jerez de la Frontera, just 30 minutes away. The airport is serviced by several low-cost airlines.

Driving Distances

Cadiz – Jerez   40 km / 25 miles

Cadiz – Seville   127 km / 79 miles

7-TARIFA

Kitesurfing in Tarifa

The wind-swept city of **Tarifa** is the southernmost city in Spain and a gateway between Africa and Europe. Tarifa is only 14 km (7 miles) north of Morocco.

Because of its unique location, world travellers have long been intrigued by this place. Phoenicians, Romans and Arabs have left their mark on Tarifa.

The meeting of the Atlantic Ocean and the Mediterranean Sea gives rise to strong winds and perfect waves, making Tarifa the wind surfing capital of Europe.

In the 80's, extreme sports aficionados discovered Tarifa. Since then this fishing village has become a favorite destination for wind and kite surfing enthusiasts, who arrive each year to participate in competitive events.

In Tarifa, winds can reach speeds of up to 80 km per hour, creating ideal conditions for powering wind turbines. Tarifa boasts a large-scale commercial wind farm with dozens of turbines.

The waters that surround Tarifa are home to resident dolphins as well as migratory whales.

In recent years, the town of Tarifa has also become a favorite spot for European digital nomads.

TARIFA ATTRACTIONS

In Tarifa, visitors will find plenty of seafood restaurants, tapas bars, long sandy beaches, whale watching boat tours and a maze of old streets for walking and sight-seeing.

Castillo de Guzman el Bueno

This impressive castle, built in 960 AD, is full of history and has played a role in the defense of the city since the time of the Moors. From this castle, visitors can enjoy great views over the port and Northern Africa.

Roman Ruins of Baelo Claudia

This ancient Roman site is located in the town of Bolonia, about 15km north of Tarifa. Visitors can stroll around the ruins and enjoy superb views of the coast.

Tarifa and Northern Coast of Africa

Getting There

The two closest airports to Tarifa are Gibraltar (40 minutes away) and Malaga (90 minutes to 2 hours). Bus service to Tarifa is available from both airports.

Driving Distances

Tarifa – Gibraltar   40 km / 25 miles

Tarifa – Malaga   159 km / 99 miles

8-GIBRALTAR

Rock of Gibraltar

Although **Gibraltar** has not belonged to Spain for some 300 years, this guide would not be complete without mentioning the town that lies on the west side of the iconic Rock.

If you happen to be near the coast, a visit to Gibraltar will make an unforgettable day trip.

Gibraltar offers gardens, caves, beaches, marinas, fine hotels, restaurants, shopping and amazing views of the Mediterranean, on the southernmost point of Europe.

GIBRALTAR ATTRACTIONS

Apes of Gibraltar

The most popular attraction in Gibraltar are the Barbary Macaques, the only wild monkey population found in the European continent.

A popular belief holds that as long as these apes live in Gibraltar, the territory will remain under British rule. These monkeys are fed a daily supply of fresh fruit and vegetables to supplement their natural diet. Feeding them is strictly forbidden.

The best place to see the apes is in the **Gibraltar Nature Reserve**, located in the Upper Rock area of the island.

Cable Car

Another main attraction is a trip on the Cable Car to the Top Station. This is the best place to enjoy magnificent views across the sea and watch the apes running wild. There's a souvenir shop at the top of the rock.

A second group of apes can be found at the **Apes Den** located at the middle station of the Cable Car.

To explore some of the Rock on foot you can ride the cable car to the top and then walk down to the Nature Reserve.

The Gibraltar Cable Car is located at the southern end of Main Street next to the **Alameda Botanical Gardens**. Reservations are not required but you will avoid long lines by arriving early in the day.

The Cable Car is open every day, seven days a week, except on Christmas and New Year's Day.

Practicalities

The **Gibraltar pound** (GIP) is the currency of Gibraltar and it is exchangeable with the British pound. British coins and bills are accepted in Gibraltar.

Since Gibraltar is a British territory, non-European visitors must show their **passport** to visit the rock. Gibraltar is rather small and **parking** may be difficult or nearly impossible at times so it's best to avoid bringing a large vehicle. Some people park their vehicle on the Spanish mainland and just walk.

Trivia

John Lennon (with Yoko Ono), Roger Moore and Sean Connery got married in Gibraltar.

How Gibraltar Became a British Territory

Soon after King Charles II of Spain died in 1700 without an heir, France and Austria began to quarrel over their legitimate rights to the throne. Eventually, war broke out, and on August of 1704, British and Dutch soldiers captured Gibraltar.

The war continued until 1713 when the Treaty of Utrecht determined that Philip V, a grandson of the king of France, would inherit the Spanish throne. As part of the deal, the treaty ceded Gibraltar to Great Britain.

During World War II, Gibraltar served as a base for the Allies to control all maritime traffic entering the Mediterranean Sea from the Atlantic.

It seems very unlikely that Britain will ever give up control of such a strategic location and most of the 32,000 residents of Gibraltar wish to remain British.

Still, Gibraltar's sovereignty remains a bone of contention and the Spanish government has, on occasion, closed the border.

Getting There

A flight from the UK takes 2 hours and 30 minutes. Visitors from other countries can fly into Malaga (the closest international airport).

Bus service runs from **Malaga** and **Tarifa** to **La Linea de la Concepcion**, on the Spanish border.

Driving time from Malaga to Gibraltar is about 90 minutes and from Tarifa, 30 minutes.

9-MALAGA

Malaga Port

Malaga, the capital of **Costa del Sol** is a thriving, cosmopolitan city with a rich history, an international airport and a busy port, where hundreds of cruise ships dock every year.

Malaga has something for everyone: An old quarter with historic sights, fine shops, museums, plenty of restaurants, tapas bars, sunshine and beaches.

Driving through Malaga, with its port, the ocean and the suburbs spreading over the surrounding hills, the views from the highway are superb.

Its public transportation system makes Malaga a good base for exploring the coast.

MALAGA ATTRACTIONS

Malaga's city centre offers plenty of sights and activities for the entire family. The following are just a few highlights.

Malaga Park

Malaga Park

An oasis during the hot summer months, **Parque de Malaga** has a large collection of plants from around the world. Visitors can enjoy shaded walks under a green canopy right in the heart of the city.

Gibralfaro Castle and the Alcazaba Fortress

This 14th century Moorish fortress offers some of the best views of the city, the port, seaside and the surrounding mountains. There's a Roman amphitheater near the fortress.

City Bus Tour

The **Hop-On Hop-Off** City Bus Tour offers narrated views of Malaga. Tickets are valid for 24 hours and allow unlimited use, meaning passengers can hop-on and hop-off as many times as they want during a 24-hour period.

Bicycle Tours

For those who want to move around a bit, a bicycle tour of Malaga provides a fun, eco-friendly way to tour the city.

Mercado Central de Atarazanas

This fresh market, located on Calle Atarazanas, not far from **Parque de Malaga**, is a great place to stop for lunch and enjoy a great variety of fresh fruits, vegetables, seafood, cheeses, tapas, spices and more.

Picasso Museum

Malaga is the birthplace of Pablo Picasso. This museum offers a collection of 200 works from the artist. Multi-lingual headphones provide explanations of the paintings. A must stop for art lovers.

Getting There

Malaga Airport

Several international carriers fly into Malaga airport, the fourth busiest airport in Spain. The Malaga airport is just 8 km from the city centre.

The train station near **Terminal T3** links the Malaga airport to the city centre and the seaside resorts of **Torremolinos**, **Benalmadena** and **Fuengirola**.

Malaga Train Station

There's another train station, called **Maria Zambrano**, located inside the **Vialia Shopping Mall**, just 4 stops away from the airport. From this station you can take a fast train to several cities including Madrid, Seville and Barcelona.

Malaga Bus Station

The Malaga **bus station** and the Maria Zambrano **train station** are located next to each other, making Malaga one of the most convenient transportation hubs in Costal del Sol.

Should I Take the Train or Bus?

That depends. When travelling from Malaga to Torremolinos, Benalmadena, Fuengirola or Mijas, take the **C1** train.

If you are heading west towards Marbella, San Pedro de Alcantara, Estepona, La Linea de la Concepcion (for Gibraltar) or Algeciras, then take a bus from the Malaga bus station.

Driving Distances

If you fly into Malaga, the following list of driving distances may come in handy when planning an itinerary.

Malaga – Nerja	56 km / 35 miles
Malaga – Marbella	60 km / 37 miles
Malaga – Ronda	105 km / 65 miles
Malaga – Gibraltar	129 km / 80 miles
Malaga – Granada	134 km / 83 miles
Malaga – Cordoba	158 km / 98 miles
Malaga – Seville	208 km / 129 miles

10-COSTA DEL SOL

The area along the coast that stretches from Gibraltar to Nerja is one of the most popular tourist destinations in southern Europe.

Costa del Sol is home to numerous expat communities attracted by its mild weather, sandy beaches, resorts and scenic villages.

Getting Around

The city of Malaga is the transportation hub for all the towns along the Costa del Sol. For tips and information on getting around please see the previous section on Malaga.

In the following pages we will visit two superb destinations along the coast.

MIJAS

Mirador of Mijas

Mijas Pueblo

Mijas Pueblo is a traditional Andalusian white village, located high on a hillside, above the town of Fuengirola.

Mijas offers reasonably priced bars and restaurants, plenty of shops and fantastic views of the sea from the **Mirador of Mijas**.

Mijas Costa

This is a nice residential community, next to Fuengirola, not very crowded with beautiful beaches and many amenities.

Due to the large number of expats who live in the area, it is easy to find English speaking businesses and medical centres in Mijas Costa.

Mijas is a great base for exploring the coast and taking day trips to Marbella, Ronda, Gibraltar and other nearby destinations.

Cala de Mijas is a pleasant seaside village west of Mijas Costa.

Playa de Calahonda is one of the best beaches in this area, with several decent bars and restaurants. Walkers can stroll on **La Cala Boardwalk** and enjoy long walks along the sea.

(Do not confuse this **Playa de Calahonda** near Mijas with the town of Calahonda near Motril or the Calahonda Beach in Nerja).

Getting There

There is no train connecting Malaga airport to Mijas Costa or Mijas Pueblo, but you can catch a train to Fuengirola, and from there take a taxi to Mijas. Shuttle transfers from Malaga airport to Mijas are fast and convenient.

NERJA

Calahonda Beach in Nerja

East of Malaga visitors will find some of the best beaches in southern Spain in a more authentic and less congested natural setting.

The town of **Nerja** provides a perfect mix of Andalusian charm, with narrow cobbled streets, tapas bars and great views of the sea, minus the crowds and congestion often seen on other beach resorts along the coast.

Nerja combines the feel of a small town with all the amenities needed for a pleasant stay, including a wide range of accommodations, plenty of bars, restaurants, supermarkets and shops.

Nerja has a large expat community so English is spoken in many places.

The **Balcon de Europa** is the first place to go to when visiting Nerja. Lined with palm trees, this scenic viewpoint is ideal for strolling and taking photographs.

Visitors can descend to the beach from both sides of the Balcon de Europa via a stairway.

Nature lovers will enjoy exploring the caves near Nerja. Nerja's caves, all individually lit, contain archaeological finds and natural stalactite formations.

Close to Nerja, tourists can visit the secluded beach of **Maro** and the white-washed village of **Frigliana** perched high on a hill above Nerja and overlooking the sea. Daily buses link Nerja to Frigliana and Maro.

Getting There

Nerja sits right on the coast, 45 km (28 miles) east of Malaga, about a 50 minute drive from the Malaga Airport. You can travel from Malaga to Nerja by taxi, minibus transfer, rental car or by bus.

There is daily bus service between Nerja and Granada, with scenic views of the Sierra Nevada and the coast. Average driving time from Granada is 2 hours by bus, depending on the number of stops.

FLAMENCO

Flamenco Street Dancer

Spaniards have music in their blood and street performers can often be seen in public places, bars and restaurants in all the main cities.

Flamenco is a genre of Spanish music and dance that originated in Andalusia and involves singing, dancing, guitar playing, hand clapping and rhythmic foot stomping.

There are many variations of flamenco and each artist imparts his or her own distinct style to this passionate art form. No two performances are alike.

I have watched back to back shows in a single evening where the same performers will improvise different songs and dance routines.

It is not uncommon to find talented street dancers and musicians performing outdoors in public places, particularly during the Summer months.

The best way to experience flamenco is by attending live shows where you can see dancers work themselves up into a frenzy of rhythm, hand clapping, fast footwork and intense emotion.

Flamenco shows usually last about 90 minutes. Ticket prices vary depending on the city and venue but they typically range between 15 to 25 euros per person.

TAPAS

Mixed Tapas

This is one thing everyone loves about Spain. Tapa literally means 'cover' or 'lid' in Spanish.

A tapa is a tasty appetizer that can be made from olives, potatoes, fried fish, pork stew, thin slices of cured ham, Manchego cheese, a slice of *tortilla* (potato and egg omelette) and much more.

Eating tapas is a social ritual where friends and family gather around a table early in the evening to share a drink and sample small bites of great tasting food.

In some parts of Andalusia (like Granada) customers get a free tapa with every drink. Some bars offer better tapas with each successive drink (a clever way of preventing customers from leaving).

Three or four tapas are usually enough to make a meal. Tapas are usually served at noon and in the evening, often until closing time or midnight.

Eating tapas is always a fun experience and a simple, inexpensive way to get a taste of Spanish culture.

GETTING AROUND ANDALUSIA

Driving through Andalusia

Andalusia highways are modern, safe and offer amazing vistas. In general, there isn't much difference between train and bus travel times, although bus fares are more economical.

Consider actual travel time when planning a day trip. On a map, Ronda may appear to be closer to Malaga than Gibraltar, however, they are both 90 minutes away from Malaga.

TRAINS

Spain has an impressive network of railways. RENFE (Red Nacional de los Ferrocarriles Españoles) connects all the major cities in the country. The trains are comfortable and well kept, with dining cars and sleeping compartments available at an extra charge. Ticket prices vary with the type of train, seat class and speed.

In general, the more stops a train makes, the cheaper the ticket. You can purchase your train tickets at train stations, through Renfe's web site or from a local travel agent.

Renfe train tickets can be purchased at several travel agencies in Spain including **El Corte Ingles** Travel Agency.

www.renfe.com

BUSES

Spanish buses are modern, comfortable, convenient and moderately priced. Bus stations offer decent dining facilities, shops, vending machines, restrooms and information booths. Some buses have bathrooms.

Buses usually make rest stops after two or two-and-a-half hours of driving. In Spain there are multiple daily trips to most cities.

Tickets can be purchased online, at a bus station through vending machines (accepting cash, credit or debit cards), or from a ticket agent. Avoid waiting in line by arriving early to the station.

www.alsa.com

ACCOMMODATIONS

Visitors will find a range of choices from simple rooms in private homes (costing anywhere from 12 to 20 euros a night) to luxury boutique hotels (about 150 euros a night). Most travellers will probably prefer something in between.

For the best prices and to insure vacancies, it is best to book online.

Booking.com - Hostels, hotels, apartments and more.

BedandBreakfast.com - World's #1 online B&B directory

Always write down the reservation or confirmation number so the hotel staff can find your booking. When making online reservations for the same day, the hotel staff may not have enough time to receive your booking.

VOLTAGE, ELECTRICITY

If you bring electronic equipment such as a laptop, digital camera or cell phone from a non-European country, make sure the charger can handle 220 voltage and get a European plug converter. AC outlets in Spain have two round holes.

To protect your computer, I recommend using a surge protector such as "Eurosurge 220V Surge Protector". This gadget is available on amazon.com and other retailers.

CYBER CAFES

A "locutorio" is a cyber café where you can use a computer, send faxes, make copies, print, scan documents and make international calls. It's like having your own office. Locutorios are fairly inexpensive.

Unlike regular businesses, these places usually stay open seven days a week, even during evenings and Holidays. (They are mostly owned and operated by foreigners).

BUSINESS HOURS

No place is perfect. In Andalusia, most businesses close at 2PM for a 3 hour *siesta*. This is something I still struggle with but perhaps having reduced business hours has helped Andalusia retain its identity.

An Italian friend of mine said it best: "Andalusia is like a lover, imperfect and with many faults. Still, I can't help loving her".

Give yourself plenty of time, energy and space to get important things done.

Banks and government offices are usually open from 9:00h to 14:00h. ATM machines work 24/7.

Some stores reopen at 17:00h after a 3 hour *siesta*. However, banks and government offices do not reopen in the afternoon.

Large department stores like **El Corte Inglés**, and supermarkets are open Monday through Saturday, except on holidays.

The main **post office** (Oficina de Correos) in large cities is usually open until 20:30h, while small offices may close at 14:30h.

On Sundays few businesses open except for bars, restaurants and souvenir shops. In the month of **August** many small businesses close for two weeks or even longer.

To ship important documents and packages overseas, contact the nearest **DHL** office.

USEFUL LINKS

www.andalucia.com – Official Andalusia Tourist Website

www.travelmath.com – Trip calculator for driving times, travel distances and more

www.renfe.com – Official site of Red Nacional de Ferrocarriles Españoles (trains)

www.alsa.com – Bus company in Spain

www.booking.com – Accommodations

www.BedandBreakfast.com – World's #1 online B&B directory

IMAGE CREDITS

Unless otherwise specified, all images and content are copyright protected and are the property of the author.

Other Attributions

I would like to thank all the photographers whose creative talent helped illustrate this book:

The Alhambra, by GFXTemplate, Pixabay

The Albayzin, by Shrutim Krishnan, Pixabay

Mezquita (Mosque) of Cordoba by James (Jim) Gordon, Wikimedia

Bridge over Guadalquivir in Cordoba by Monika Wojnowska, Pixabay

El Tajo de Ronda y el Parador de Turismo by Pedro J Pacheco, Wikimedia

Kitesurfing in Tarifa, by perszing1982, Canstockphoto

Emergente, Tarifa by Basilievich, Wikimedia

Apes of Gibraltar by Lee Cassam, Pixabay

View of Malaga Port by Gzzz, Wikimedia

Spanish mix of tapas by Michal Osmenda, Wikimedia

ADIOS FOR NOW!

Thank you for joining me on this tour of Andalusia.

With more than 1000 white villages dotting out the landscape of Andalusia, you're bound to come across some incredible scenery. Allow some time for rest stops, sightseeing and some unplanned adventures.

I hope you've found this book useful and enjoyable.

Happy travels!

Liz Marino

ABOUT THE AUTHOR

Liz Marino has travelled and lived in Andalusia since 2010. She enjoys writing useful, concise guides to help readers get the information they need fast. Liz is an English teacher and a freelance translator.

CPSIA information can be obtained
at www.ICGtesting.com
Printed in the USA
LVHW070829290119
605621LV00027B/859/P